Weird But True Weather

WEIRD BUT TRUE SCIENCE

Carmen Bredeson

Series Science Consultant:
Mary Poulson, PhD
Biologist
Central Washington University
Ellensburg, WA

Series Literacy Consultant:
Allan A. De Fina, PhD
Dean, College of Education/Professor of Literacy Education
New Jersey City University
Past President of the New Jersey Reading Association

CONTENTS

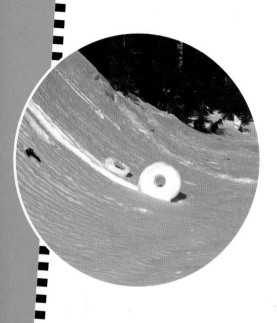

Words to Know   3

Weird Weather   4

Hailstones   7

Snow Donuts   8

Rain   11

Strange Clouds   12

Sundogs   15

Dust Devil   16

Mirages   19

Fulgurites   20

Learn More

    Books   22

    Web Sites   23

Index   24

WORDS TO KNOW

 **fulgurite (FUHL guh riyt)**—Melted sand made by lightning.

 **hailstone (HAYL stohn)**—Ball of ice that falls from a cloud.

 **mirage (muh RAHJ)**—Air waves that make you see something that is not really there.

 **ripples (RIH puhlz)**—Little waves on the top of the water.

WEIRD WEATHER

Weather causes many weird things to happen on Earth. Have you ever seen strange weather? Turn the page and get started reading about weird but true weather!

What Causes Weather?

Water is always moving. It goes from Earth to the sky and back to Earth. Some water is rain. Other water falls as big chunks of ice! This water cycle has a lot to do with weather. Hot air and cold air change the weather, too.

HAILSTONES
HARD BALLS OF ICE

Most **hailstones** are the size of peas or small marbles. But sometimes softball-sized hail comes crashing down. Take cover! It could knock you out. Hail that size breaks windows and smashes crops in the fields.

It's weird, but it's true!

SNOW DONUTS

GET OUT OF THE WAY!

A small snowball starts rolling downhill. It picks up more and more snow and rolls faster. Soon it is a giant ball. Wind blows the soft middle away. A snow donut is left, speeding down the hill.

It's weird, but it's true!

RAIN

THIS WATER FELL ON DINOSAURS!

Rain falls on you. Rain fell on the dinosaurs.
It might be the same rain. Water on Earth is used over and over. It is called the water cycle. Sun heats the water. It rises to make clouds and rain. It's the SAME water that has always been here!

It's weird, but it's true!

STRANGE CLOUDS
FLOATING MYSTERIES

Is that a flying saucer in the sky? No, it is just a lenticular (len TIK yoo lur) cloud. Strong winds blow over a mountain. They swirl and twist the clouds. Some of the clouds look like they came from outer space!

It's weird, but it's true!

Sundogs

Which one is real?

Are there THREE suns in the sky? No!
The smaller spots on each side of the sun
were made by pieces of six-sided ice in the air.
The ice bends the sun's light. The bent light
causes you to see the bright spots on each side
of the sun.

It's weird, but it's true!

DUST DEVILS

GET OUT THE VACUUM CLEANER.

Here comes a dust devil! It forms when hot air rises into cooler air above. The hot air begins to turn. It picks up dust and dirt as it spins across the ground.

It's weird, but it's true!

MIRAGES
WHAT'S THAT UP AHEAD?

Throw a rock into water. **Ripples** move across the water. **Mirages** are like ripples in the air. Sometimes a dry road up ahead looks wet on a hot day. This is a mirage. The air above the road gets hot from the sun. This air has ripples in it.

It's weird, but it's true!

FULGURITES
TWISTING TUBES IN THE SAND

Lightning strikes the sand. BAM!
The hot bolt of lightning snakes through the ground.
Sand around the lightning melts. The melted sand cools.
Hard tubes of sand are left behind. They are in the shape
of a lightning bolt.

It's weird, but it's true!

LEARN MORE

Books

Dickstein, Leslie. *Time For Kids: Storms!* New York: Harper Collins, 2006.

Harris, Caroline. *Science Kids: Weather*. New York: Kingfisher, 2009.

Slade, Suzanne. *How Do Tornadoes Form?* Mankato, Minn.: Picture Window Books, 2010.

LEARN MORE

Web Sites

NOAA. Weather for Kids.

http://www.crh.noaa.gov/gid/?n=weatherforkids

University of Illinois. Tree House Weather Kids.

http://urbanext.illinois.edu/treehouse

The Weather Channel Kids!

http://www.theweatherchannelkids.com/weather-center

INDEX

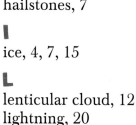

D
dinosaur, 11
dust devil, 16

E
Earth, 4, 11

F
fulgurite, 20

H
hailstones, 7

I
ice, 4, 7, 15

L
lenticular cloud, 12
lightning, 20

M
mirage, 19

N
rain, 4, 11
ripple, 19

S
snow donut, 4, 8

sundog, 15

W
water, 11
water cycle, 4, 11, 19

To our wonderful grandchildren: Andrew, Charlie, Kate, and Caroline

Enslow Elementary, an imprint of Enslow Publishers, Inc.
Enslow Elementary® is a registered trademark of Enslow Publishers, Inc.

Library of Congress Cataloging-in-Publication Data
Bredeson, Carmen.
Weird but true weather / Carmen Bredeson.
  p. cm. — (Weird but true science)
Includes index.
  Summary: "Find out about ball lightning, snow donuts, mirages, hailstones and other weird weather events"—Provided by publisher.
ISBN 978-0-7660-3862-2
1. Weather—Miscellanea—Juvenile literature. I. Title.
QC981.3.B722 2011
551.6—dc22
                            2010035863
Paperback ISBN: 978-1-59845-372-0

Printed in China

052011 Leo Paper Group, Heshan City, Guangdong, China

10 9 8 7 6 5 4 3 2 1

To Our Readers: We have done our best to make sure all Internet Addresses in this book were active and appropriate when we went to press. However, the author and the publisher have no control over and assume no liability for the material available on those Internet sites or on other Web sites they may link to. Any comments or suggestions can be sent by e-mail to comments@enslow.com or to the address on the back cover.

Photo Credits: Associated Press, pp. 2, 9; © De Agostini Editore/Photolibrary, p. 10; Gopherboy6956/Wikipedia, p. 14; © iStockphoto.com/Ales Veluscek, pp. 3 (hailstone), 6; NASA/Visible Earth, p. 4; Photo Researchers, Inc.: © Chase Studio, p. 20, © Kent Wood, p. 3 (mirage), 18, © Peter Menzel, p. 3 (top), 21; Shutterstock.com, pp. 1, 3 (bottom), 13; Tom LaBaff, p. 5.

Cover photo: JC/WN/GES/WENN.com

Note to Parents and Teachers: The *Weird But True Science* series supports the National Science Education Standards for K–4 science. The Words to Know section introduces subject-specific vocabulary words, including pronunciation and definitions. Early readers may need help with these new words.

Enslow Elementary
an imprint of
Enslow Publishers, Inc.
40 Industrial Road
Box 398
Berkeley Heights, NJ 07922
USA
http://www.enslow.com